THE SEVEN WONDERS OF THE ANCIENT WORLD

BY ERIN ASH SULLIVAN

P9-BIE-617

TABLE OF CONTENTS

INTRODUCTION

People today make "best of" lists of all kinds—the top 40 songs, the 10 best movies, and so on. Even in ancient times, people made such lists. One of these lists was "The Seven Wonders of the Ancient World."

The Seven Wonders were all large, human-made structures. Some were built to honor the dead. Some were built to honor gods, goddesses, or a special occasion. One was built for pleasure and one was built for a very practical purpose.

As you read about the Wonders, you will learn why they were wonderful. You will find out what they were used for. You will also learn how we know about them today, even though six of the seven are no longer standing.

The Great Pyramid is the only one of the Seven Wonders still in existence today.

TIME LINE OF THE SEVEN WONDERS

2560 B.C. Great Pyramid of Giza is built

This is the Lighthouse at Alexandria. A Dutch artist drew this picture of the lighthouse after he read a description of it.

What is fact and what is **myth**, or possibly made up, about the Seven Wonders? When **archaeologists** study ancient civilizations, it's hard for them to know things for certain. But they look for clues that can help them solve the mysteries of the past. As you read, think about how archaeologists make their best guess as to what is true and what is made up. Ask yourself also if the Seven Wonders remind you of any structures in today's world.

600 B.C. Hanging Gardens of Babylon are built

550 B.C. First Temple of Artemis is built at Ephesus

353 B.C. Mausoleum at Halicarnassus is built

285 B.C. Lighthouse at Alexandria is built

450 B.C. Statue of Zeus at Olympia is created

300 B.C. Colossus of Rhodes is created

HISTORY OF THE WONDERS

S everal ancient **historians** wrote "Wonders of the World" lists. The most famous list was made by a Greek historian named Herodotus (her-AW-duh-tihs). Herodotus traveled around the Mediterranean Sea. The sights he saw led him to create the list of Seven Wonders used in this book.

THE SEVEN WONDERS

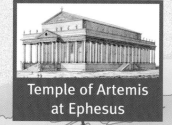

Temple of Artemis at Ephesus

GREECE

Aegean Sea

ASIA MINOR (TURKEY)

Ephesus

Olympia

Halicarnassus

Rhodes

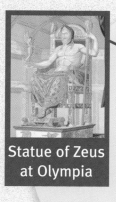

Statue of Zeus at Olympia

M e d i t e r r a n e a n   S e a

Alexandria

Giza

EGYPT

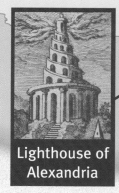

Lighthouse of Alexandria

Nile River

statue of Herodotus

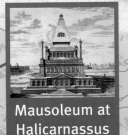

Mausoleum at Halicarnassus

Tigris River

Euphrates River

BABYLONIA (IRAQ)

Colossus of Rhodes

Babylon

Hanging Gardens of Babylon

Great Pyramid of Giza

Without machines to do the heavy work, many people were needed to build the Wonders.

When the Seven Wonders were built, people had only simple tools to use. A lot of work had to be done by hand. That's part of what made the Wonders so amazing. Today, when people build large structures, they have all kinds of special tools and technology to make the work easier.

Today's buildings are made of a variety of materials. The people who built the Seven Wonders did not have steel or glass or concrete. They used mostly stone and mud bricks. The architects did not have modern measuring tools, calculators, or computers to help them plan. It's a wonder that the Seven Wonders were built at all.

It took many years to build each of the Seven Wonders. By comparison, it took 16 months to build the Empire State Building in New York City. The Empire State Building is one of the world's tallest skyscrapers. It has 102 floors and is 1,250 feet (381 meters) tall.

Artisans, workers with special skills, played an important part in the completion of the Wonders. They were the painters and sculptors who added the beautiful artwork to the Wonders.

IT'S A FACT

Ancient builders and artisans were known for their use of precious metals and stones. Sometimes they carved ivory or melted gold for large statues. Artisans also worked with small objects, such as jewelry.

Ancient Egyptian artisans created these treasures. The piece of jewelry above is made with beautiful stones. The chest on the left is painted with pure gold.

THE SEVEN WONDERS OF THE ANCIENT WORLD

THE GREAT PYRAMID OF GIZA

The Great Pyramid of Giza was built near the Nile River in Egypt. It is more than 4,500 years old. At 449 feet (137 meters), the Great Pyramid stands as tall as a 50-story building. For over 4,000 years, it was the tallest human-made structure on Earth.

The Great Pyramid is by far the oldest of the Seven Wonders. It is the only one still standing. It looks very different today than when it was built. When it was new, its sides were smooth and covered with gleaming white stone. That covering has been worn away by centuries of desert winds. And some of the outer stone was carried away bit by bit to be used in other buildings.

the Great Pyramid of Giza

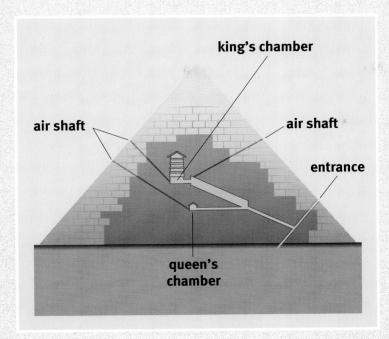

king's chamber

air shaft

air shaft

entrance

queen's chamber

Khufu's mummy was hidden in a secret chamber inside the Pyramid. But by the time archaeologists got there, grave robbers had already stolen the mummy.

The Great Pyramid was the burial place for an Egyptian ruler, or **pharaoh**, named Khufu (KOO-foo). Greek historians called him Cheops (KEE-awps). As with other pharaohs, the body of Khufu was preserved as a **mummy** after his death. His mummy was placed in a **sarcophagus**, or coffin, before burial in the Pyramid. Workers sealed the mummy of Khufu inside the Pyramid, along with food and valuable possessions.

Egyptians believed a person's spirit lived on in the body after death. So they buried people with the things they would need in the afterlife.

WHO WAS KHUFU?

We don't know very much about the pharaoh Khufu, except that he probably reigned for about 23 years around 2500 B.C. The only image we have of him is a tiny ivory statue about 3 inches (7.5 centimeters) tall.

One thing that makes the Great Pyramid wondrous is its size. At its base, it is about as big as 10 football fields. There are more than two million stone blocks in the structure, and each block weighs at least two tons, or 4,000 pounds (1,814 kilograms). The blocks used to fit so closely together that you could not fit a knife blade between them.

The measurements of the Great Pyramid are very exact. Without using modern measuring tools, the ancient Egyptians created a structure whose four sides are almost the same. The difference between the longest and the shortest sides is less than eight inches (21 centimeters)!

HERE COMES THE SUN

Archaeologists believe that the Great Pyramid's shape is tied to the Egyptians' sun god, Re (RAY). They think that the diagonal lines of the Pyramid represent the rays of the Sun hitting Earth.

The blocks of the Great Pyramid have crumbled over time. They no longer fit as closely together as they did when the Pyramid was built.

This Egyptian wall painting shows a husband and wife farming their land.

Archaeologists have many different ideas about how the Great Pyramid was built. Some think that the Egyptians built a series of ramps around the Pyramid. Workers might have dragged the huge stones up giant ramps. Or workers might have used levers or rollers to push and pull the enormous blocks up the ramps and into place.

Herodotus wrote that it took 100,000 men 20 years to complete the Great Pyramid. But archaeologists don't know if that is true. At one time, many archaeologists believed that the Great Pyramid was built mostly by slaves. Now some believe that many of the workers were farmers. During the flood season, they couldn't work on their farms, so perhaps they worked on the Great Pyramid. The workers were fed and housed in a special village built just for them. Archaeologists have found the remains of a village that housed up to 20,000 people.

This engraving was based on descriptions of the Hanging Gardens of Babylon.

THE HANGING GARDENS OF BABYLON

Mystery surrounds the Hanging Gardens of Babylon (BA-buh-lahn). Why were they built? What did the Gardens look like? The little information we have comes from descriptions by ancient Greek and Roman historians.

Supposedly, Babylonian King Nebuchadnezzar (neh-buh-kuhd-NEH-zuhr) built the Gardens around 600 B.C. near his palace in the city of Babylon. Historians believe he built them for his wife who missed the green mountains of her homeland, Persia. Workers brought in trees and plants and placed them on high **terraces**. These terraces were flat platforms that rose up like steps. Plants hung over the edges of the terraces, which may have given the Hanging Gardens their name. Ancient historians said they looked like a lush, green mountain rising up out of the desert.

How could such beautiful gardens exist in that hot, dry desert? Some ancient historians believe the Gardens must have been built near the Euphrates River. The ancient **engineers**—people who design structures—probably used the river to irrigate, or water, the plants.

But how did they get the water up to the terraces? The ancient Greek geographer, Strabo, wrote that: "Persons . . . are continually employed in raising water from the Euphrates into the garden."

The water might have been lifted to the top of the Gardens by a chain of buckets hauled by workers. It could then run down through channels built into the Gardens and keep the soil moist.

No Babylonian writings about the Gardens have yet been found. So no one knows for sure how the Gardens worked.

The ruins of Babylon can be found in modern-day Iraq.

Around 1900, an archaeologist guessed that the Babylonians used a chain-pump system of pulleys and buckets to irrigate the Hanging Gardens.

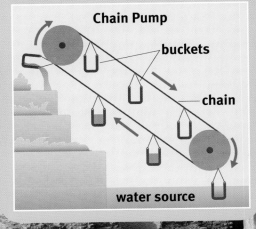

Chain Pump

buckets

chain

water source

THE STATUE OF ZEUS AT OLYMPIA

If you were a Greek citizen 2,500 years ago, you would have wanted to go to Olympia. This valley was one of the most important sacred, or religious, places in ancient Greece, full of temples to gods and goddesses. Most of the temples were quite bare and simple. Often, the statue of the god or goddess was the only thing inside.

At Olympia, you could have admired the Temple of Zeus, king of the Greek gods and goddesses. Then you could have entered the temple and stood before the statue of Zeus. Ancient writers said that it made visitors feel as if they were in front of the great god himself.

The enormous statue was completed around 460 B.C. It was taller than a three-story building and showed Zeus seated on a throne. Legend says the head of the statue was so close to the roof of

In this artist's version of the Statue of Zeus, the god is holding the Greek goddess Nike in one hand and a royal scepter, or stick, in the other.

This sketch shows the height of the statue in relation to an average sixth-grade student.

the temple that Zeus would take the roof off if he tried to stand up.

The statue's size and its precious materials made it a Wonder. Zeus's skin was made of ivory, and his clothes and beard were made of gold. His throne was covered with ebony and precious stones. A marble pool in front of the statue held olive oil. Workers spread oil on the ivory to protect it from the damp air.

After worship of Greek gods was banned, the Temple of Zeus was closed. The statue was later moved to the city of Constantinople (kahn-stan-tehn-OH-pahl)(now Istanbul, Turkey) by wealthy Greeks. The statue was destroyed by fire in A.D. 462.

POINT

MAKE CONNECTIONS

Look at the photo of the Lincoln Memorial in Washington, D.C. How is it like ancient Greek temples?

Lincoln Memorial

THE TEMPLE OF ARTEMIS AT EPHESUS

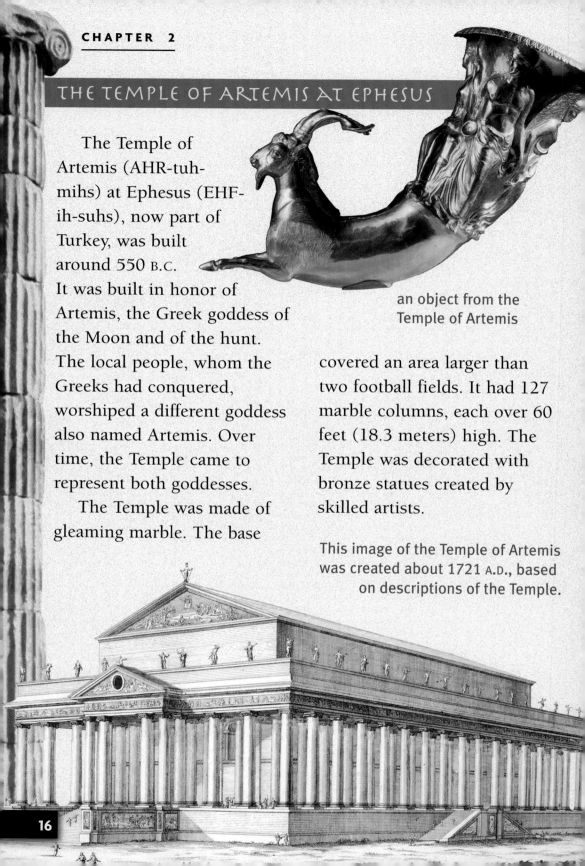

The Temple of Artemis (AHR-tuh-mihs) at Ephesus (EHF-ih-suhs), now part of Turkey, was built around 550 B.C. It was built in honor of Artemis, the Greek goddess of the Moon and of the hunt. The local people, whom the Greeks had conquered, worshiped a different goddess also named Artemis. Over time, the Temple came to represent both goddesses.

The Temple was made of gleaming marble. The base

an object from the Temple of Artemis

covered an area larger than two football fields. It had 127 marble columns, each over 60 feet (18.3 meters) high. The Temple was decorated with bronze statues created by skilled artists.

This image of the Temple of Artemis was created about 1721 A.D., based on descriptions of the Temple.

For a while, Ephesus was a bustling, wealthy city, and the Temple was its chief attraction. The Temple was a place for worship and for trade. But then the region became part of the Roman Empire. Many people stopped worshiping the Greek gods and goddesses and avoided the Temple. It was finally destroyed by a group of invaders, called the Goths, in A.D. 262.

In the 1800s, archaeologists **excavated** the site. Today, you can see the ruins, including some of the pillars. To see the rest of this amazing building, you would have to use your imagination.

ruins of the Temple of Artemis

IT'S NUMBER ONE?

Antipater (an-TIHP-eht-er) of Sidon was a Greek poet and writer who lived about 2,500 years ago. He is another person who made a list of the Seven Wonders. He claimed that the Temple of Artemis put all the other human-made wonders "in the shade."

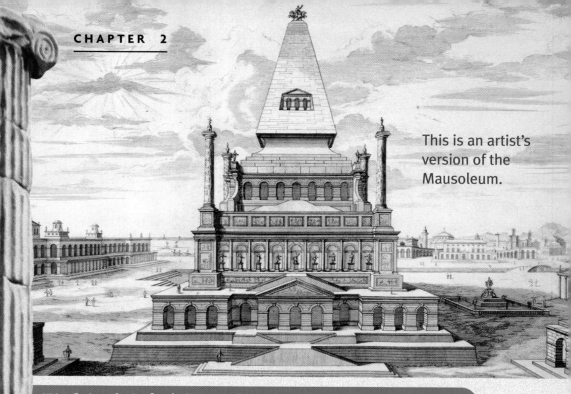

This is an artist's version of the Mausoleum.

THE MAUSOLEUM AT HALICARNASSUS

King Mausolus (maw-SOH-luhs) ruled from 377 to 353 B.C. in what is now Turkey. A grand tomb was built in the city of Halicarnassus (ha-lih-KAHR-nuh-sihs) to house his body after death. A new word was created as well: **mausoleum**. The word comes from Mausolus's name and refers to any large tomb.

Most archaeologists believe this to be the statue of Mausolus from the top of the tomb.

FACT OR FICTION?

Some ancient writers said that Mausolus's queen had the mausoleum built after her husband's death in 353 B.C. But it was finished in 350 B.C., and it's hard to believe that it took only three years to build. Many historians believe that Mausolus himself started the project while he was alive.

The huge square burial chamber was carved by four of the best artists of the day, one working on each side. According to written descriptions, the tomb looked like a Greek temple, with columns and statues all around. Stone lions guarded the structure. The top was 140 feet (43 meters) above the ground, and featured a statue of a horse-drawn chariot.

Inside, the ashes of the king and queen lay in golden caskets. The walls had carved sections called **friezes**. The friezes showed scenes from ancient history and myths.

Earthquakes damaged the mausoleum in the 1200s. Then in the 1500s, people finished the damage. They took the stones away to strengthen a nearby castle. The stones are still in the castle walls today. Archaeologists have explored the site of the mausoleum and found some of the sculptures and friezes.

This mausoleum is in Central Park in New York City. It was built as a tomb for President Ulysses S. Grant, who died in 1885.

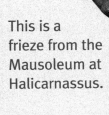

This is a frieze from the Mausoleum at Halicarnassus.

THE COLOSSUS OF RHODES

About 2,300 years ago, the people of Rhodes, a Greek island in the Aegean (ih-JEE-ehn) Sea, were ready to celebrate. They had defeated an invading army. To honor their sun god, Helios, they decided to build a monument. That is how the **Colossus**, or huge statue, of Rhodes came to be.

The people of Rhodes melted down equipment left behind by the defeated army. They used the metal to build a colossus about 110 feet (33.5 meters) high. The hollow statue was supported with stone columns and iron beams on the inside. The outside was bronze. The statue stood on a 50-foot (15-meter) **pedestal**, or base. As the statue got higher and higher, the workers built up mounds of dirt to stand on so they could reach the top.

This amazing structure took 12 years to complete. When it was finished, workers dug away the mounds of dirt. The statue stood tall, blazing in the Sun. According to descriptions, it wore a crown upon its head. It might have held up a torch in one hand.

The Colossus stood for only 56 years before it collapsed in an earthquake. But one man who saw it after it fell wrote, "Even lying on the ground, it is a marvel."

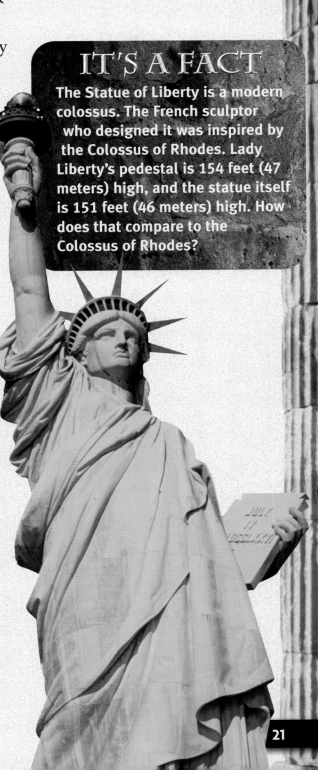

IT'S A FACT

The Statue of Liberty is a modern colossus. The French sculptor who designed it was inspired by the Colossus of Rhodes. Lady Liberty's pedestal is 154 feet (47 meters) high, and the statue itself is 151 feet (46 meters) high. How does that compare to the Colossus of Rhodes?

Artists can only imagine what the Colossus looked like. Based on descriptions, some artists imagined that he straddled, or spread across, the city's harbor. This would have made it difficult for ships to travel in and out. Modern archaeologists believe that the statue was probably standing at the entrance to the harbor.

THE LIGHTHOUSE OF ALEXANDRIA

The Lighthouse of Alexandria was built around 285 B.C. It stood in the harbor of Alexandria, Egypt. The land around the harbor was flat. That made it hard for sailors to spot the land from out at sea. The Lighthouse was used to guide ships safely into port.

How did the Lighthouse work? Near the top was a huge mirror made of polished bronze. It reflected sunlight. At night, a fire was built in the Lighthouse. Historians think that the mirror might have given the firelight extra power by reflecting it. The light could be seen from ships 35 miles (56.3 kilometers) away.

IT'S A FACT

The Lighthouse of Alexandria came to be known as Pharos, (FAR-ahs) after the island on which it was built. It was so famous that the words for *lighthouse* in French, Italian, Portuguese, and Spanish come from the word *pharos*.

These images of the Lighthouse were made by two different artists.

What made the Lighthouse such a wonder? It was very tall, nearly as tall as the Washington Monument, which is about 550 feet (167 meters) tall. White marble covered the surface of the Lighthouse. On its top stood a statue of Poseidon (puh-SIGH-duhn), the Greek god of the sea. One myth tells how the Lighthouse mirror, reflecting the blazing rays of the Sun, was used as a weapon to set enemy ships on fire.

Earthquakes in the 1300s reduced the Lighthouse of Alexandria to rubble. People used its marble blocks in other buildings. The bronze mirror was probably melted down to make coins. But we know what the Lighthouse looked like because its image appeared on coins of the time.

In the mid-1990s, divers explored the harbor of Alexandria and found stone blocks that might have been part of the Lighthouse.

✓POINT

REREAD

Reread the descriptions of the Seven Wonders. Look for similarities and differences among them.

FROM ANCIENT TO MODERN

An Ancient Wonder Survives

The only surviving Wonder is the Great Pyramid of Giza, the oldest of the Seven Wonders. Several facts help explain why this 4,500 year-old structure still stands. With its broad base, the Pyramid is stable. So unlike some of the other Wonders, it could withstand earthquakes. The desert climate is dry, so rain has not worn away the Pyramid's stones. Unlike other Wonders, it has not been destroyed by fire or completely taken apart by people.

But the Great Pyramid has not survived undamaged. Some of its treasures have been lost to thieves. And desert winds as well as air pollution play a part in wearing away some of the stones.

A scientist prepares a robot to explore an air shaft in the Great Pyramid.

IT'S A FACT

Five thousand tourists visit the Great Pyramid every day. They are hurting the Pyramid—just by breathing! Their breath leaves salt in the air, and the salt causes cracks in the stone.

Archaeologists don't always work outside at a site. Sometimes they study samples in a lab. Other times they work in a library or office to gather information or write about their findings.

HISTORICAL PERSPECTIVE

Many of the ancient Wonders were explored by archaeologists from other parts of the world. Some of these scientists brought statues, paintings, and other artifacts back to their own countries to study and display in museums. What do you think of this behavior?

Archaeologists are now working with the government of Egypt to protect the Great Pyramid. They are repairing some of the damage to the structure. They are trying to limit the number of tourists who visit the Great Pyramid and the smaller pyramids at Giza. To prevent damage from car exhaust, the Egyptian government is not allowing cars to get too close to the Pyramid.

Modern Wonders

Are there any modern, human-made wonders? There are many! But remember: what makes something wondrous or not is a matter of opinion.

The Petronas Towers might be called a wonder. Built in 1998 in Kuala Lumpur (KWAH-luh loom-POOR), Malaysia, these towers are the tallest buildings in the world. They are made of high-strength modern materials and rise to 1,483 feet (452 meters). Slender and graceful, they are truly a wonder of modern design and construction. By comparison, the Empire State Building is 1,250 feet (381 meters) tall and Chicago's Sears Tower is 1,454 feet (443 meters) tall.

the Petronas Towers

THE FIRST SKYSCRAPER

The first modern skyscraper was the Home Insurance Building in Chicago, Illinois, built in 1885. It was only 138 feet tall, or 10 stories! Now many city buildings are much taller than that. But at the time, it towered above the buildings around it.

The Aswan Dam could be another modern wonder. Built in Egypt in 1970, this huge dam controls flooding on the Nile River. It is more than two miles long and rises 364 feet (111 meters) above the riverbed. Water from the dam is used to produce electricity for hundreds of thousands of homes and businesses.

Another of today's possible wonders lies under water. It's called the "Chunnel," or the "Eurotunnel." The Chunnel is a railway tunnel that runs beneath the English Channel and connects France and England. Opened in 1994, the Chunnel is 31 miles (50 kilometers) long, and is about 150 feet (46 meters) beneath the ocean floor. Using the Chunnel, high-speed trains can cross the English Channel in just 20 minutes—at a top speed of 186 miles per hour!

The lake formed by the Aswan Dam is called Lake Nasser.

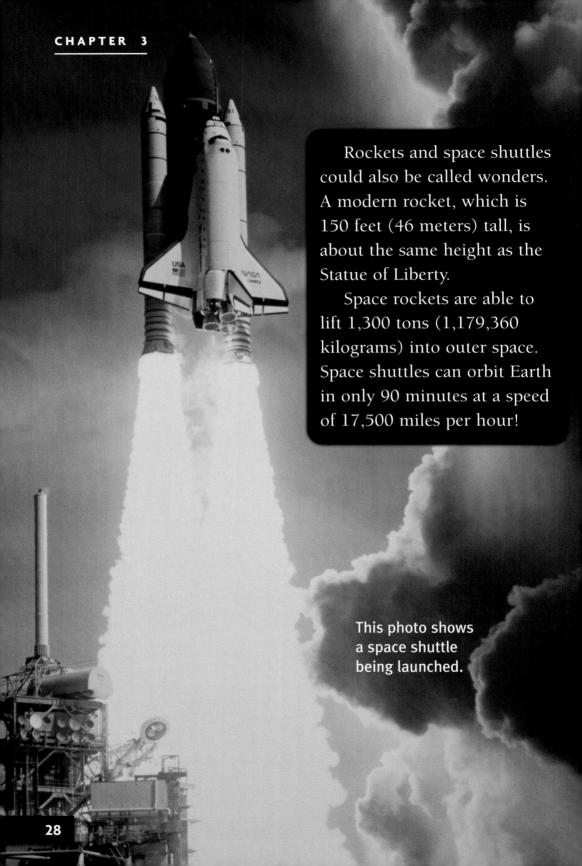

Rockets and space shuttles could also be called wonders. A modern rocket, which is 150 feet (46 meters) tall, is about the same height as the Statue of Liberty.

Space rockets are able to lift 1,300 tons (1,179,360 kilograms) into outer space. Space shuttles can orbit Earth in only 90 minutes at a speed of 17,500 miles per hour!

This photo shows a space shuttle being launched.

CONCLUSION

Just like writers today, writers in ancient times wanted to amaze their readers with tales of wonderful things. That is probably how Herodotus's list of Seven Wonders came to be.

The Wonders changed over time as they collapsed, burned, or were taken apart.

Only one Wonder from the list remains: the Great Pyramid of Giza. With some help from its protectors, the Pyramid might survive for many more years.

If the Seven Wonders were built today, many people would not find them amazing. But in their day, built without the use of modern technology and materials, they were wondrous indeed.

Like the Hanging Gardens of Babylon as shown in this artist's version (left), the gardens at the Getty Center (below) in Los Angeles, California, grow in terraces.

The Seven Wonders of the Ancient World show us that ancient peoples created things that were amazing and beautiful, as people do today. Then, as today, people celebrated religion, wealth, and power in their monuments.

The Seven Wonders of the Ancient World connect us to the past. They also remind us that we must work to protect and save the best parts of our own culture. Even the grandest of human-made monuments, left unprotected, can crumble away.

These glass-and-steel pyramids are part of the Louvre (LOOV) museum in Paris, France.

the Great Pyramid

GLOSSARY

archaeologist (AHR-kee-AHL-uh-jihst) a scientist who studies an ancient civilization by looking at its structures and artifacts (page 3)

artisan (AHR-tuhs-uhn) a skilled worker (page 7)

colossus (kuh-LAW-suhs) a huge statue (page 20)

engineer (ehn-juhn-EER) a person who designs machines or buildings (page 13)

excavate (EHKS-kuh-vayt) to dig up (page 17)

frieze (freez) the decorated walls, or surfaces, of a building (page 19)

historian (hihs-TOHR-ree-uhn) a person who studies the past (page 4)

mausoleum (maw-suh-LEE-uhm) an impressive, grand tomb (page 18)

mummy (MUH-mee) a preserved body (page 9)

myth (mith) an old story that deals with heroes or ancestors (page 3)

pedestal (PEH-duh-stuhl) a stand or base for a statue (page 20)

pharaoh (FEHR-oh) an ancient Egyptian king (page 9)

sarcophagus (sahr-KAWF-ah-guhs) a decorated stone coffin (page 9)

terrace (TEHR-uhs) a flat platform that can be placed on top of another flat platform of larger size (page 12)

INDEX